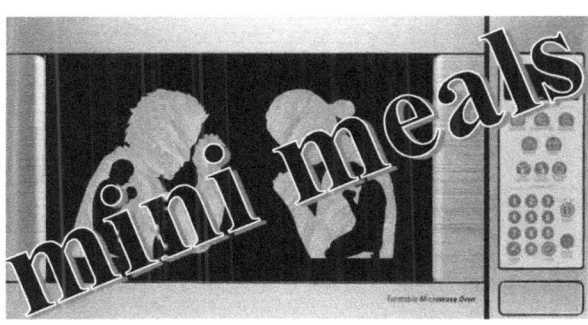

Cooked On The Outside
Raw On The Inside

The Struggle to Wait on God's Timing

Second Edition

Cooked On The Outside

Raw On The Inside

The Struggle to Wait on God's Timing

Second Edition

Ken Bosket

Copyright Information

Copyright© 2022 by Ken Bosket
Unless otherwise indicated, all scripture quotations are taken from the Holy Bible, King James
Version, which is open to public domain.
Scripture taken from the New King James Version (NKJV) ®.
Copyright ©1982, by Thomas Nelson. Used by permission.
All rights reserved.
Scripture referenced from www.biblegateway.com.© *1995–2017,*
The Zondervan Corporation. All rights reserved.
All rights reserved, including the right to reproduce this book or portions thereof in any form whatsoever.
ISBN: 9798218027421
Copy Editor: Dayema Woodall-Bosket
K&B Information Services Platform
www.cookedontheoutside.com
cookedontheoutside@gmail.com

To all who poured into my life, especially my wife, Dayema, who helped me believe that all things are possible through Christ, who strengthens me.

A special "shout out" to the next generation, whose impatience motivated me to write this shortened version of my original book.

Contents

Preface			11
Introduction			13
Chapter 1	The Head Chef		15
Chapter 2	Food Prep		17
Chapter 3	Appetizers		19
Chapter 4	Soup		21
Chapter 5	Salad		23
Chapter 6	Main Course		25
	Entrée #1	The Promised Meal	27
	Entrée #2	Bless My Food	31
	Entrée #3	Choosing a Meal	35
	Entrée #4	Feast or Famine	39
	Entrée #5	Dessert in the Desert	45
	Entrée #6	A Guide for Good Food	49
	Entrée #7	No More Bread	53
	Entrée #8	Anointed Meal	57
	Entrée #9	A Challenging Meal	63
	Entrée #10	Delayed Service	69
	Entrée #11	Waiting for the Feast	73
	Entrée #12	Feast for a King	77
	Entrée #13	Get Up and Eat	79
	Entrée #14	No Food in Sight	83
Chapter 7	Dessert		89
Chapter 8	Check and Gratuity		93
Chapter 9	Food for Thought		97

Preface

Why do I have to wait so long, and why can't I have it now? Some of us may have said this to ourselves at one time or another. Let's be real. Waiting for anything in today's society is tough. For the most part, we can have what we want when we want it. We live in a society dominated by social media, gaming apps, and same-day/next-day delivery services. As much as you and I enjoy technology, it has created an environment that promotes a "got to have it now" mentality. With technology making it harder and harder to wait for anything, is it possible that the answer to our prayers depends on our willingness to wait on God?

This *Mini Meals Edition* of my original book, *Cooked on the Outside, Raw on the Inside,* is designed for today's fast-paced society. It summarizes various accounts of God's past relationships with individuals in a way that quickly captures the reader's interest.

Hopefully, this book will help readers understand that delays do not mean their prayers have been denied. Come have a seat at the dining-room table (it won't be long) as we engage in a fascinating conversation about God's timing.

Introduction

One day, while sitting in a restaurant waiting for the main course, some friends and I feasted on rolls, soup, and salad. Then, still hungry, we topped it all off with some appetizers. After some time had passed, we were full. Then I felt convicted as I looked to blame somebody for my pre-dinner eating binge.

Finally, the waitress showed up with the main course, and I was frustrated, not just because of the delay but because I was already stuffed. As she stood there with my entrée, I humbly looked at her, forced a smile (I knew it was not her fault), and stated the only three words that came to my mind, "Doggie bag, please." The main course looked great, but the timing of its delivery was off.

Similar to some dining experiences, we may feel somewhat discouraged when God's timing does not meet our expectations. I believe expectations are part of the foundation of our faith. They allow us to activate faith when God has yet to reveal His plans. I have no problems with expectations. Yet when my hopes are delayed, for a lengthy period of time, the wait can be challenging.

So how do we balance our attention-challenged, fast-paced lifestyles with our relationship with a Holy, Living God who moves at His own pace? This is the dilemma I face (and I am sure some of you do too) as I maintain a closer walk with God in our microwave society.

> So how do we balance our fast-paced lifestyles with a Holy, Living God who moves at His own pace?

The meal plans for our lives have been established and are prepared within specific parameters to satisfy the "Head Chef's" goals. Undercooked or overcooked meals are unacceptable. No matter how long we must wait, none of us wants our meals to be *cooked on the outside but raw on the inside.*

The preparation process may take some time, but let's try not to be impatient; the main course is on the way!

CHAPTER 1

The Head Chef

The Head Chef oversees all aspects of the dining experience. He is responsible for determining the menu items and food to create the perfect meal. He makes sure that all food preparations work within His guidelines and specifications. He monitors overall efficiency and verifies the quality of the food served. He listens to all requests and responds in a timely manner. His creativity is unmatched, and His ability to make something from nothing is extraordinary. He works twenty-four hours a day and seven days a week.

> The Head Chef's creativity is unmatched, and His ability to make something from nothing is extraordinary.

When He starts something, He finishes it. The meals He creates are designed explicitly for His customers. He knows their desires and focuses on their needs. A lot of thought and preparation goes into creating our promised meals. His meals may take some time to complete, but He promises to satisfy everyone's cravings.

He is the One True and Living God. "I am the bread of life. He who comes to me shall never hunger, and he who believes in me shall never thirst" (Jn. 6:35 NKJV).

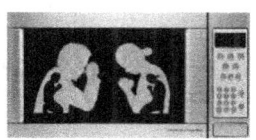

CHAPTER 2
Food Prep

It would be around the holidays, and I would smell the aroma as soon as I opened the door. I couldn't wait to see what was cooking on the stove. The average holiday meal in my home consisted of sweet potatoes, baked macaroni and cheese, rice and beans, fried chicken, baked chicken, ribs, ham, and three types of vegetables. It was my favorite time of the year.

I enjoyed the anticipation of knowing that a feast was being prepared. It was the expectancy of walking into my home surrounded by mouth-watering aromas. In fact, it was the type of cooking that brought everyone together. It was a family affair!

Is it possible that all the technological advances we have experienced over the past few decades have adversely affected today's family traditions? Just like rushing our food to cook in the microwave oven, immediate gratification has become the cornerstone of our society. If we cannot have it now, many of us will find alternative means of getting what we want.

> Just like rushing our food to cooking the microwave oven, immediate gratification has become the cornerstone of our society

I believe individuals today are challenged with creating boundaries for themselves that will allow more balance between their personal gratification and spiritual development. However, I also believe God understands the dilemma we face as we try to discipline ourselves and develop guidelines to enhance our spiritual lives.

The prep work has been completed, and the anticipation to eat is overwhelming. While waiting for the main meal, we need something to curb our appetites.

This is a good time for some appetizers.

CHAPTER 3

Appetizers

How many of you know that a good appetizer can set the tone for a main course? I am not a fan of fancy appetizers served at various upscale eateries. Just give me some chicken wings, sweet-and-sour meatballs, barbeque rib tips, or crab cakes, and I am good to go.

As I try to understand God's timing, I rationalize that maybe He operates in stages, the same way dinner is served at a restaurant. After all, the formal dining experience we enjoy today has been created and proven over time. Similar to a chef who plans his or her meals, I believe God develops specific menus for our lives. But God's meal plans require patience on our part.

It is challenging for me to wait for anything. I do not like waiting to be seated in a restaurant. If the wait is more than fifteen minutes, I am already planning my exit. I also don't particularly appreciate waiting in lines in stores. If too much time passes while I wait to purchase an item, I contemplate putting it back on the shelf and walking out. My mentality is that if management really wanted my money, they would open another register.

Maybe I shouldn't beat myself up too badly over my inability to be patient in today's microwave world. There is a reason patience is a "fruit of the spirit" (Gal. 5:22-23). For some, like me, patience does not come naturally; it is an attribute developed over time. Combine the absence of patience with a fast-paced, in-your-face society, and you have individuals (like myself) who lack tolerance for a variety of life experiences.

> Understanding that God's timing supersedes my timing is a spiritual dilemma that I am constantly grappling with.

Understanding that God's timing supersedes my timing is a spiritual dilemma that I am constantly grappling with. God may provide an immediate response to my request when necessary, but I am coming to terms with the fact that some of His main courses are slow-cooked.

The appetizers were tasty, yet this segment of our meal is only a preliminary phase of our dining experience. Sit back and enjoy; our soup is on the way.

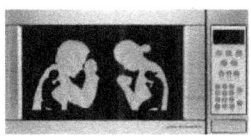

CHAPTER 4

Soup

I believe soup is another element of the dining experience that sets us up for the main meal. Besides, it is a good way to keep us somewhat satisfied until the entrée arrives.

I once met a brother who was a doorman for a high-end luxury apartment building. It turned out that he had some stories to tell. One day a tenant came out of the building and asked him to hail a taxi for her. As any professional doorman would do, he went out into the street and held out his hand to grant her request.

Unfortunately, after some time had passed, not one cab stopped for him. Frustrated with the time it took the doorman to hail a cab, the tenant stormed into the building and reported him to management. Well, it did not take long before the building's owner approached the doorman, cursed him out, and reminded him that his tenants expected executive accommodations and exceptional services. After being reprimanded, he returned to his post.

The next day, the same tenant approached the doorman and told him that she needed to get on a bus. There was not a bus stop in view. Nevertheless, he saw the serious expression on her face and knew he had to do something. When an approaching city bus was just about to pass the building, he stopped the bus by running into the middle of the street and standing directly in front of it. Then he waved to the woman, and she boarded the bus. Once aboard, he stepped aside, and the furious bus driver and passengers resumed their trip. Talk about expectations.

> How do we manage our wants so they do not lead to spiritual frustration?

In a get-it-now society, this tenant expected to be treated exceptionally, and with some help from the building's owner, her wishes were granted. She wanted what she wanted when she wanted it. Her demands were met in the natural realm, but satisfaction may not be as instantaneous in the spiritual realm.

How do we manage our wants so they do not lead to spiritual frustration? The answer may be in our ability to live by faith and trust that God's word is true.

We've had our soup, but the promised meal has yet to arrive, leaving us hungry for more. It is time to dig into our salad.

CHAPTER 5
Salad

Some of us like it, and some of us don't. Because of its properties, salad beneficially curbs our appetite until the main meal arrives. It has an abundance of fiber and other nutrients necessary for the proper functioning of our bodies. However, as far as I am concerned, salad has one critical mission: to do whatever it can to keep me from getting hungry. While waiting for the main course, let's review some promises referencing God's timing.

Biblical scholars estimate that there are approximately three thousand to eight thousand promises from God in the Bible. The way I see it, the more promises, the better. The biblical book of Timothy states, "All Scripture is given by inspiration of God and is profitable for doctrine, for reproof, for correction, for instruction in righteousness" (2 Tim. 3:16).

Now let's combine this scripture with Numbers 23:19, which states, "God is not a man that He should lie; neither the son of man that He should repent; has He said, and shall He not do it or has He spoken and shall He not make it good?"

Therefore, we know God's promises are guaranteed by a righteous God who cannot lie. Whether it is three thousand or eight thousand promises, I am holding on to all of them, trusting that God will keep His word.

A salad prior to the main meal can be important when it comes to controlling our cravings. However, despite its many benefits, it is no substitute for the main meal. Some of us may feel that waiting for God's promises takes too long. We must try to remember that our salad, along with this season of our lives, is only one portion of a greater dinner plan, a plan that the Head Chef specifically designed to satisfy our cravings.

> Some of us may feel that the wait, for the arrival of God's promises, is taking too long.

Clear away the salad bowl — the main course is arriving!

CHAPTER 6

Main Course

The main meal has arrived, specially prepared according to our tastes and uniquely created to satisfy our desires. It is served in a way that will allow us to enjoy our food and dining experience.

A couple of years ago, my wife and I went to a high-end New York City restaurant. The décor and atmosphere were exceptional. The lights were set in a soft, dim glow. My wife and I could barely read the menu, but I smoothly brushed it off and acted as though I were used to this type of environment.

After a couple of minutes of straining to see the menu, my wife got fed up. She took out her cell phone, turned on the flashlight, and aimed it toward the menu to order her food. Talk about attracting attention. The menu and the table lit up.

I ignored the glances of those dining next to us and supported her actions. My wife did what she had to do to enjoy her dining experience. After saving the evening with conversation because the service and food were not that good, I paid the bill and left.

The outside of the restaurant was beautiful, and the dining area looked exquisite, but the food and service did not meet our criteria of a high-end establishment.

> But in faith, I believe the appointed meals created for my life will always be cooked to perfection.

Like cooking food in a microwave oven, sometimes the experience of dining out may not live up to our expectations. But in faith, I believe the appointed meals created for my life will always be cooked to perfection.

With that stated, fourteen spiritual mini-meals are on the way. I am hopeful that each entrée will give us a better understanding of God's timing.

ENTRÉE #1

The Promised Meal

Not long ago, I planned to speak with my mother about possibly downsizing in favor of a smaller home. I thought her current house was too big for her to maintain. First, I talked to my sister about my concerns, and she responded with two words, "Good luck."

As I walked toward Mom's house, I knew this would be a tough conversation. After all, she had lived in that house for almost forty years. Nevertheless, I had it all planned out. I would start our discussion smoothly and build a strong case as the evening progressed.

I entered the living room, and we started to talk. I expressed to my mother the benefits of moving to a smaller residence, the advantages of not having to perform major maintenance on the house, the comfort of not walking up a flight of stairs, and the money saved from less utility costs. I strategically made my case and, just to add some spiritual spice, tossed in some scripture to bolster my defense (Don't judge me; you'd do it too). I was ready.

The conversation started nicely, my mother listened to me as a courtesy, but her expression changed somewhere during my presentation. What I was trying to get her to do must have hit her all at once as she boldly stated, "I am not moving at my age!"

Now there was an uncomfortable silence in the room as she looked at me, and I looked at her. It was a stare-down, for which I knew she had the upper hand. After all, I may have been her son, but I was in her home, and she had the final say. Speaking only those seven last words, she shut that topic down and left the room.

Looking back, I can understand my mother's reluctance to move. Even if the move in the long hall would be beneficial, the energy and time it takes to make such a move would be overwhelming.

Unlike my mother, a man named Abraham had a destiny that could only be fulfilled if he relocated from his home. Only an act of faith could cause a seventy-five-year-old man to obey God's command, pack up his things and his family, and relocate to "the land I will show you" (Gen. 12:1). Now that is faith, because initially God did not even tell Abraham the name of the land that Abraham would be was going to.

Abraham and his wife, Sarah, had no children; however, God told Abraham to "look now toward heaven and count the stars if you are able to number them ... So shall your descendants be" (Gen. 15:5 NKJV). It sounded good, yet ten years after God's promise,

Abraham was still waiting for his child to arrive. As he got older, I can only guess that his patience ran out, and his frustrations started to get the best of him. Maybe Abraham was concerned that he was getting up in age and wondered whether God remembered His promise.

Abraham decided to take things into his own hands at eighty-six years old. He slept with his wife's maid and had a son named Ishmael. It was a decision made outside of God's will, and even though God was faithful to forgive him, there is always a price to pay for disobedience.

As a consequence of his actions, Abraham had to wait fourteen more years before God's promise was fulfilled. Abraham was one hundred years old, and his wife was ninety when Isaac, their promised child, was finally born. I believe God made the odds even greater to prove that he could make the impossible possible.

Abraham's experience reveals the struggle between our desires and God's plans for our lives. Even with Abraham's failure to wait on God's timing, God kept His word and allowed him to give birth to another child — one chosen by God. Talk about an encouraging story! There is not much we can do to supersede the will of God. We can do things our way or do things His way.

> **There is not much we can do to supersede the will of God. We can do things our way or do things His way.**

The Head Chef's meals are made to order and cooked to perfection. He designs them to be served at the appropriate time. Meanwhile, we must try to be patient; more promised entrees are on the way!

ENTRÉE #2

Bless My Food

A couple of years ago, my coworker and I had a conversation about the hard work that goes into preparing food for the Christmas holiday. She said she had double the work because her family would start celebrating the night before Christmas. She would cook an entire meal on Christmas Eve and do it again on Christmas Day. I looked at her and asked, "Why would you cook the night before a major holiday?" She looked at me, smiled, and said, "It's tradition."

My family is from the South, and I was unaware of traditions that would have you prepare a feast twice for a holiday. As far as I am concerned, Christmas dinner is enough work. What my mother did not cook, family members cooked and brought to the gathering. The rule of three was the foundation for our holiday dinners: no less than three meats, three vegetables, three starches, and three desserts. Any additional dishes were an extra blessing.

Scripture reveals that a man named Jacob was a cook in his own right. However, unlike my co-worker, who cooked for her family with love, Jacob used his cooking skills to deceive and exploit those closest to him. His manipulation of his twin brother was so severe that it set off a chain of events that would affect his family for generations to come.

Twin brothers, Esau and Jacob, had been fighting since birth. Esau was an Alpha male, skilled hunter, and "man of the open country." Jacob was happy just to be home, hanging out in the tents (Gen. 25:27). Today, he probably would be considered a momma's boy.

Now it does not take a therapist to figure out what happens when a parent favors one child over another. Isaac (the father) loved Esau, and Rebekah (the mother) loved Jacob (Gen. 25:28). This split within their family produced a sibling rivalry that took a nasty turn for the worse.

One day, while Jacob was home cooking a meal, his brother came in from hunting and was starving. Jacob decided to take advantage of the situation. Although they were twins, Esau was born first and was eligible to receive the largest portion of his family's inheritance.

In an opportunistic moment, Jacob offered his brother, Esau, food in exchange for Esau's inheritance. So much for brotherly love! To make things worse, Jacob held the food as a bargaining chip and watched Esau starve until Esau swore his inheritance to him (Gen.

25: 29–34).

With his future and legacy at stake, Esau made a horrible decision. He chose to eat the food Jacob offered him in exchange for his inheritance. It was a mistake that would haunt Esau for the rest of his life. Delighted, Jacob got what he wanted, but unfortunately for Esau, Jacob was not done. He wanted more!

Being fooled once was enough, but Esau got cheated a second time when he was to receive a spiritual blessing from his father, Isaac. Again, Jacob double-crossed Esau by stealing his identity (he pretended to be Esau) and tricking Isaac into giving him the spiritual blessing that belonged to Esau. Realizing that he had lost everything, Esau had enough and vowed to kill his brother, Jacob. Fearing for his life, Jacob left home to stay with his Uncle Laban until Esau cooled off.

> Esau had to choose whether to satisfy his hunger or give up his inheritance.

Twenty years (look at God's timing) after running away from his brother, the Head Chef revealed Jacob's meal plan. The same underhanded Jacob who cheated his brother out of his birthright and blessing would receive the promise God gave to Abraham: "I will multiply your descendants as the stars of the heaven and as the sand which is on the seashore" (Gen. 22:17 NKJV).

It took over two decades, but despite Jacob's flaws, God used him as an unlikely source to fulfill His promise. If the Head Chef can take scraps of food from Jacob's life and create a meal that would be a blessing to others, then He can surely bless us with a feast that will cleanse our hearts and restore our rightful position at His dinner table.

That is a meal worth waiting for!

ENTRÉE #3

Choosing a Meal

She was the eldest of two sisters. Her name means "weary", which could indicate that she had some sort of childhood ailment. Scripture states that she was "tender-eyed," which may suggest that her eyesight was weakened (Gen. 29:17). She was beautiful in the eyes of God, but in the eyes of man, her appearance left a lot to be desired. On the other hand, her younger sister Rachel was beautiful, attractive, and Jacob desired to have her as his wife. Unfortunately, life was about to become complicated for both women.

It was time to celebrate. The marriage celebration was underway and continued throughout the evening. Laban brought his daughter to Jacob in the middle of the night, But in the morning, when the sun rose on Jacob's home and he was able to see clearly, Jacob was livid and stunned. The woman beside him was not his lovely, beautiful Rachel but her elder, tender-eyed sister, Leah (Gen.

29:25).

Distraught, Jacob confronted Laban about why Leah was in his bed. Laban told him it was customary for the eldest daughter to be married first. While Jacob struggled to come to terms with his predicament, Leah was also coming to terms with the fact that she was married to a man who did not love her.

One cannot imagine what was going through Leah's mind as Jacob confronted her father about their marriage. Rejection, humiliation, embarrassment, and hurt are some words one could probably attribute to Leah's state of being as she waited for Jacob to return home.

> Despite her predicament, God had a purpose for Leah's life.

Despite her predicament, God had a purpose for Leah's life. She needed a breakthrough, but she had to wait on God's timing. How does one wait on God's timing when the pain, hurt, and grief initiated from one's suffering seems to challenge an individual's faith? "Rest in the Lord, and wait patiently for him: fret not thyself because of him who prospered in His way" (Ps. 37:7).

Leah may have been unloved by Jacob, but God loved her. It was not long before God blessed Leah by allowing her to have children, but Rachel's womb was closed (Gen. 29:31). Scripture could not have made the results of God blessings for Leah any clearer. Altogether, Leah had six boys and one girl from Jacob, but that was only the beginning of a timed series of events that would fulfill God's redemption plan for the world.

Because Leah dared to praise God during her pain, a special meal was created for her life. No longer would her legacy be remembered as scraps of love placed on her plate by her husband. What Leah thought was an uncooked meal hastily served to her ended up being a feast. One that birthed a lineage through her fourth child, Judah, which produced our Lord and Savior, Jesus Christ.

Leah's meal started with crumbs but ended up becoming a dish that was cooked to perfection!

"I will not tell you that I fully understand God's timing, but I do recognize that God sees the bigger picture."

ENTRÉE #4

Feast or Famine

My mother had a great relationship with a dedicated member of our church. This member moved to Florida and prayed daily for her granddaughter in New York, Janet, whom she had not heard from in months. She told my mother she was concerned about her granddaughter and was praying for a breakthrough. Fearing the worst, she asked my mother if I could assist in locating her granddaughter.

Now, I am far from an investigator, nor do I like wandering the streets looking for someone, but for some crazy reason, I agreed to help. The next thing I knew, I was in my car headed to some unknown address in New York City. I pride myself on adapting to any situation, but I was unprepared for this. After all, asking too many questions in someone's neighborhood can lead to severe consequences. Nevertheless, I proceeded with the little faith I had that Janet would be found.

I hesitantly drove up the block toward a building complex. My first stop was a community center, where no one knew who Janet was or recognized her name. Then I walked into the lobby of one of the apartment buildings and began looking for her name on mailboxes. After five minutes, I abruptly dropped that idea as tenants started looking suspiciously at me. After exiting the building, I saw a mail carrier delivering mail. This was the break I needed.

He would probably know most of the tenants residing in the neighborhood. I did not want to follow him into the building, so I waited for him by his truck. Fifteen minutes later, the mail carrier and a few other people walked out of the building. When he arrived at his truck, I asked whether he knew Janet Devas. He stated no, but just then, a woman walked by.

She stopped while looking at me suspiciously and asked, "Did you say Janet Devas?" I replied yes. Her eyes scanned me from top to bottom, and then she said, "What business do you have with Janet?"

Amazed, I responded, "I just wanted to relay a message for Janet to give her grandmother a call." After staring at me for a minute, she replied, "I know Janet; she is my niece." I said to myself, *Yes*!

I asked her if she would have Janet call her grandmother as soon as possible. She gazed at me cautiously and said she would relay the message. Then she walked away.

As I headed toward my vehicle, I asked myself, *What is the probability of questioning people in a community center and reading random names on mailboxes, only to stand in the street and mention Janet's name at the exact time her aunt was walking by?*

I can only surmise that God's timing is perfect, and He still hears the prayers of the righteous. "The effectual fervent prayer of a righteous man availeth much" (Jm. 5:16). Though my search was challenging, Janet got her message, and I learned a valuable lesson about trusting God's timing.

> I can only surmise that God's timing is perfect, and He still hears the prayers of the righteous.

Scripture notes that at seventeen, a young teenage shepherd, Joseph, was taking care of his family's flocks. Joseph was his father's (Jacob's) favorite son. God revealed to Joseph in a dream that he would rule over his whole family. How many of us know that some revelations should not be shared with others? Without any filtering and probably with some youthful arrogance, Joseph told his family the details of his dream (Gen. 37). It did not take long before he was scolded by his father and hated by his brothers.

One day Jacob sent Joseph outside to search for his brothers. His brothers saw Joseph arriving from a distance and plotted his demise. He was favored by their father, had dreams of ruling over them, and that concept was too much for Joseph's brothers to handle. They jumped Joseph, tied him up, and did the unthinkable — sold him into slavery.

Joseph became a slave to Potiphar, an Egyptian who was one of Pharaoh's (ruler of Egypt) officials. Joseph was away from his father and alone in a foreign land. He probably thought he had seen the worst that could ever happen in his young life; however, Joseph had no clue of what was coming next.

> Joseph probably though he had seen the worst in life, but he had no clue what was coming next.

Sometime during his captivity, Potiphar's wife made sexual advances toward Joseph. However, Joseph was a man of integrity, and when he refused to sleep with his master's wife, she accused him of sexual harassment and had Joseph thrown into prison. Sold into slavery and now imprisoned, how long could Joseph hold onto the hope that everything would work out, considering time was not on his side?

Thirteen years later, the Pharaoh of Egypt was experiencing distressing dreams that none of his magicians or wise men could decipher. Joseph was known in prison to have a gift for interpreting dreams and was summoned to appear before Pharaoh. Through God's divine revelation, Joseph listened and accurately interpreted Pharaoh's dream — a feat none of Pharaoh's advisors could do.

Astonished, Pharaoh told Joseph, "You shall be over my house, and all my people shall be ruled according to your word; only in regard to the throne will I be greater than you" (Gen. 41:30–41 NKJV). Joseph was thirty years of age when he became second in command to Pharaoh and governor over all of Egypt.

I will not sit here and tell you that I fully understand God's timing. Nor will I pretend that waiting thirteen years for one's deliverance is easy, but I do recognize that God sees the bigger picture and knows what's best.

> I will not tell you that I understand God's timing, but I do recognize that God sees the bigger picture.

Joseph did not know it, but amid confusion and chaos, his designated meal plan was in effect. It was only after he was granted the position as Governor of Egypt that he realized the true meaning of his dream at seventeen (Gen. 42:9). It took some time to take effect, but in God's timing, Joseph was restored to his rightful place at the Head Chef's table.

What an amazing story of a meal that was cooked and timed for victory!

"They say time heals all wounds. Sometimes I am not too sure, but I do believe time allows the healing process to begin."

ENTRÉE #5

Dessert in the Desert

He was a beautiful baby boy abandoned by his mother, not because she didn't love him, but because she wanted to save his life. He was found by the edge of the shoreline not far from an Egyptian palace. He was born a Hebrew but raised in a royal household. One could say he was in the house but not of the house.

Growing up, he experienced the finer things of life. He was sheltered from the day-to-day difficulties that affected his people. The plight of his people always disturbed him. When Moses was forty years old, he witnessed an Egyptian attacking a Hebrew. He was devastated by this incident, took matters into his own hands and killed the attacker. News of the Egyptian's murder reached Pharaoh, and he immediately called for Moses' death.

Moses knew he was in trouble and realized that he had to make a move. He managed to escape Egypt and Pharaoh's wrath. He once lived in a palace, but now he was a fugitive with nowhere to go. He might have had second thoughts about killing the Egyptian. Maybe he could have handled the situation differently. However, the damage was done, and now he had to deal with the consequences of his actions.

They say time heals all wounds. Sometimes I am not too sure, but I do believe time allows the healing process to begin. During this grim season of Moses's life, there seemed to be a pattern developing, revealing his compassion for the oppressed. It may ultimately be the trait that would thrust him into his God-given destiny.

> Whether he knew it or not, God's purpose was playing a major role in his life

When Moses was eighty years old, God remembered the covenant He made with Abraham, Isaac, and Jacob (Ex. 2:24). I do not know why it took so long, but it is still comforting to know that God does not forget His promises. Moses was living his life and was unaware that God was setting the stage for him to play a major role that would set His people free.

Revealing Himself through a burning bush, God told Moses that he would be the one to lead His people to the Promised Land. I love how God described the land He had prepared for His people. He broke it down in terms they could understand and described it as the "land flowing with milk and honey". It does not get any better than that!

After some deliberation, Moses reluctantly agreed to lead God's people as long as his brother, Aaron, could accompany him. Now the stage was set. Forty years after he ran from Egypt, Moses was on his way back to demand that Pharaoh release His people, Israel.

Moses and Aaron were now standing in front of Pharaoh, boldly stating that the Lord wanted Pharaoh to let His people go. Pharaoh denied their request, and God, seeking to demonstrate that He was in control, sent ten plagues that would devastate Pharaoh and the Egyptian people (Ex. 7:5).

Pharaoh's stubbornness prevailed through nine plagues; however, the tenth plague was the ultimate blow. God allowed the firstborn child of every Egyptian household to die. Finally, a defeated Pharaoh freed the children of Israel and allowed them to leave Egypt.

The first forty years of Moses's life reflected parts of an incomplete meal that was not ready to be served; however, the second half revealed a plan that ensured that Moses's main course was ready to be consumed. Yes, it did take some time, but God kept His promise. He said He would deliver His people, and He did it!

As you will see in the next entree, acknowledging a promise is one thing, but acquiring a promise is another story.

"I am gradually learning to accept the fact that there are things I am not supposed to understand."

ENTRÉE #6

A Guide for Good Food

My future wife and I had been dating for approximately three months. She asked me what was my favorite meal. I am neither a foodie nor a picky eater, so I told her my favorite dish was chicken Caesar salad. I could have made things interesting and told her barbeque chicken, collard greens, baked macaroni and cheese, and cornbread. However, I wanted to keep it simple, so a chicken Caesar salad with real shredded parmesan cheese would suffice. She promised that she would prepare my favorite meal someday soon. One month later, as we continued to date and the relationship strengthened, I remembered her promise and asked her about my chicken Caesar salad. She was working on some critical projects at the time and asked me to be patient. I readily responded, "No problem."

Months later, things were looking up. God was working in her life and mine, so what better time to ask her about my chicken Caesar salad, right? Well, I cannot describe the look on her face when I brought up the topic. She looked at me regretfully and stated that her projects were near completion and that she would make my chicken Caesar salad in two weeks.

Dinner night was here, and I was ready to enjoy my meal. I called her prior to driving to her house, but she did not pick up her home phone. Then I called her on her cell phone. She picked up, paused, and apologetically stated that due to some unanticipated work obligations, she was not able to prepare for our dinner date. Now I was not only disappointed but also frustrated and hungry.

After grudgingly discussing the situation with her, she asked me to please come by her home anyway. Because it was late, she said she would purchase dinner for us and promised to cook my chicken Caesar salad in a couple of weeks.

Still somewhat disappointed, I hesitantly agreed to meet her at her home. While we ate dinner, she gave me a more detailed explanation as to why the evening did not go as expected. The atmosphere was cordial, and the food turned out to be pretty good. Things may have started out a little rough, but in the end, it turned out to be an enjoyable dinner date.

By the way, two weeks later, she finally made me my homemade chicken Caesar salad, and it exceeded my expectations. It was great. Good things do come to those who can wait. But did it have to take so long?

Evidently, waiting on my chicken Caesar salad was far easier than learning how to wait on God's promises. As I get older, I am slowly learning to accept the fact that some of God's promises may require action on my part. These are steps of faith He may expect from me when His purpose is in the process of being implemented.

I am not saying that God needs me to fulfill His promises, but I believe that I personally play a role in a spiritual equation that requires an activation of faith (Jm. 2:17). I do not fully understand the relationship between God and man, but I do know that the spiritual equation works. I am gradually learning to accept the fact that there are things I am not supposed to understand.

> Waiting on my chicken Caesar salad was far easier than learning to wait on God's timing.

As the Israelites were on the precipice of entering the Promised Land, twelve scouts were secretly sent out to examine its resources. When they returned, they reported that the land was rich in soil and fertile enough to grow various crops. However, they also noted that the people who lived there were big, strong, and resided in massive cities.

Ten scouts, who explored the land, got scared and spread discouraging information about the Israelite's ability to obtain the land. By the time they finished telling their story, the Israelites were terrified. They had no faith, vision, or confidence that God would conquer their giants.

In a rallying-the-troops moment, two scouts, Caleb and Joshua, told the Israelites that the land was tremendous and God would give them victory. But the Israelites were not hearing it, and it was not long before they picked up stones to kill Caleb and Joshua. Just before they could throw one stone, God intervened, stopped the potential onslaught, and punished the Israelites for their lack of faith.

> Although God promised the land to the Israelites, Moses was required to conquer it as a test of faith.

Amid the turmoil and chaos, God remembered Caleb and Joshua. He especially honored Caleb's faithfulness and willingness to trust Him. Caleb took a stand for God, and God rewarded him. He promised Caleb that he would not be affected by the punishment given to the Israelites.

Caleb was forty years old when he initially scouted the Promised Land and was eighty-five when he crossed into it. Scripture states that Caleb was not weakened, physically or mentally, by the wait. (Josh. 14:10–11).

Caleb finally entered the Promised Land, and I finally got my chicken Caesar salad. God is good!

ENTRÉE #7

No More Bread

A couple of years ago, our family suffered the untimely death of a family member. He was young and in the prime of his life. He loved the Lord and served on the marriage ministry at his church. We knew his spiritual fate was secure, but at that moment the sting of death seemed to override everything. It was not long before the question arose, "Why would God allow a spiritual brother to die at such a young age?"

We still wrestle with this question today. It coincides with the reflective question, "Why do bad things happen to good people?" In my layman's effort to understand these types of unexpected occurrences, I sat down one day and reasoned that there must be a spiritually sound answer. After all, I believe nothing just happens.

I take it that original sin, initiated by Adam and Eve, is the reason why believers and nonbelievers can suddenly be affected by unfortunate circumstances. Scripture states, "Therefore, just as through one man sin entered the world, and death through sin, and thus death spread to all men, because all sinned" (Rom. 5:12 NKJV).

The first man's disobedience to God seemed to introduce inescapable consequences that adversely affected all future generations. "Nevertheless, death reigned from Adam until Moses, even over those who had not sinned in the likeness of the transgression of Adam, who is a type of Him who was to come" (Rom. 5:14 NKJV).

> **The first man's disobedience introduced inescapable consequences that adversely affected all future generations.**

The scriptures alone note the devastating effect of original sin on humanity. Yet I am encouraged to know that even death has no victory in the end. "And God shall wipe away all tears from their eyes; and there shall be no more death, neither sorrow, nor crying, neither shall there be any more pain: for the former things are passed away" (Rev. 21:4). Although the death of my young brother saddened me, I am comforted to know that God is still in control.

I read about two women who persevered through horrible circumstances and were brought back to their destinies through divine intervention. Their story is an example of God working all things for good, even when their circumstances seemed to be spiraling out of control.

Naomi was married and had two sons. Food was scarce in Bethlehem, so in order to seek provisions for the family, Naomi and her husband relocated to Moab. Just when they were getting settled in their new home, Naomi's husband died. In a microwave minute, she lost the head of her household, the provider for her children, and the protector of her family.

Years later, more enjoyable times ensued when Naomi's two sons got married. Both of her sons' wives, Oprah and Ruth, were natives of the area. For the next ten years, Naomi and her family lived in Moab. The foundation of a new family structure was being established. She was in a new season — a season of optimism, hope, and boundless possibilities.

Some say that lightning does not strike twice, but Naomi's situation was an exception to the rule. Scripture gets right to the point and does not mince any words describing the next tragedy that took place. Naomi's two sons died suddenly (Ru. 1:5).

Naomi decided that she had enough, and it was time to go back to her home. Oprah decided to return to Moab, but Ruth chose to stay with Naomi. Ruth refused to give up on Naomi, and in a statement that could melt the heart of anyone, Ruth told Naomi, "For wherever you go, I will go; and wherever you lodge, I will lodge. Your people shall be my people, and your God, my God. Where you die, I will die, and there will I be buried" (Ru. 1:16–17 NKJV). Now that is a commitment!

Resources were scarce as Naomi and Ruth settled in Bethlehem. In an effort to obtain food, Ruth took the initiative to gather some leftover grain from a field. When the field's owner Boaz saw her, he had compassion for her and allowed her to harvest not just from the leftover grain but also from the premium grain.

> Boaz's response is a reminder that God does not forget the good that we do.

Seeing that Boaz would be a good match for Ruth, Naomi educated Ruth on her culture and what she needed to do to find marital favor with him. Ruth took Naomi's advice and gracefully made it known to Boaz that she was interested.

This story ends like a made-for-television romance movie. Boaz ends up marrying Ruth, and they were blessed with a son named Obed. Ruth's son, Obed, became the father of Jesse. Jesse was the father of David, and David was of the lineage of our Lord and Savior, Jesus Christ (Ru. 4:17). Whether or not we understand the Head Chef's meal plan, His timing is always perfect, even if the food is hard to swallow.

What an amazing story regarding a meal that seemed to be raw on the inside, but ended up being cooked and served with perfection!

ENTRÉE #8
Anointed Meal

    Several years ago, I was an electronic technician working indoors. I wanted to take me experience to the next level, so I decided to interview for a field technician position. This position was a step up in salary and opportunities, but I knew that working in the field would be stressful. I would have to be in my car traveling from company to company, repairing equipment. When a service call comes in, you have to respond in a timely manner. This job promised to take me out of my comfort zone, but I believed I was ready for the challenge.

    My prospective employer was a Fortune 500 company located in New York. I was praying for the best and was ready for the worst. I knew everything about the company, including the highs and lows of its stock. I rehearsed my responses to essential questions that the interviewer might ask me. I was dressed in one of the few suits I wore to church. I found a briefcase and placed all my interview documents along with some other stuff in it to look impressive. I was ready.

During the interview, I could tell the manager was pleased with my presentation. The conversation flowed nicely from the beginning to the end. When it was all over, I shook his hand, and while I was headed toward the door, I heard him say, "Please follow me," as he walked into another room. I mumbled to myself, noting that this could not be good.

Inside the room was a working model of their electro/mechanical processing unit. The manager told me that he would simulate some of the problems that may arise if I worked in the field. He stated that I had four attempts to repair the unit and that I must get at least three out of four attempts correct.

The manager told me to wait outside as he rigged the unit until it was inoperable. He then called me in and told me to repair it. As I walked into the room, I asked (allright, I begged) God for a miracle. Thankfully, I was off to a good start.

My first two attempts to repair the unit were successful. The third attempt did not go well. Now I needed to fix the unit one more time to get the job. I took my jacket off as sweat started to trickle from my forehead. As the manager walked out of the room one last time, he told me, "Good luck."

I knew he was being nice, but I needed more than luck to make this happen; I needed divine intervention. I entered the room and began to troubleshoot. After attempting to fix the unit for what felt like forever, I finally had to admit the unavoidable truth — I was lost.

I had no idea how to get this unit to work. I adjusted every linkage and still could not get it to function properly. After looking up and shaking my head toward God as though it were His fault, I called the manager in and stated, "I'm done." He did not know how true those words were.

I sat in the back of the room while he tested the unit. Minutes had passed, and he still did not tell me what I already knew: the unit was not working. After a lengthy period of time, he stood up, turned to me with a disturbed look on his face, and stated, "I don't know what you did or how you did it, but the unit is working."

What? It was a hallelujah moment!

With a smile on my face and a false sense of swag, I packed my stuff and was ready to walk out of the door. Then with a curious voice, he asked me, "Can you show me what you did?

No! My inner voice shouted. *You have got to be kidding.*

So I put my stuff down and proceeded toward the unit. Now telling him that it was the favor of God was not going to wash with this manager. He wanted an explanation.

I slowly began by rambling troubleshooting techniques off the top of my head. In desperation, I focused on the drive unit, explained its function, and rotated the drive belt until it came to a complete stop. With a convincing voice, I looked him in the eyes and said, "See? It works."

He looked at me confused and stated, "Yes, it certainly does work." I stood up, grabbed my stuff, and waited there as he stared at the unit, trying to comprehend what had just occurred.

Finally, he shook my hand as we walked out and stated that I should expect to hear from him soon. I walked out of the office exhausted but grateful, knowing God somehow worked this out for my good. By the way, I got the job, but the process was not what I'd expected it to be.

As with my experience during the interview, a young man named David learned that the road to destiny could have unexpected bumps and potholes. I learned this lesson the hard way as I struggled to complete the practical portion of my interview. On a grander scale, David faced the unexpected as he struggled to obtain the anointed meal that the Head Chef had destined for his life.

> David learned that the road to destiny could have unexpected bumps and potholes.

He was the youngest of eight boys born to his father, Jesse. David, a teenager, was responsible for caring for the family sheep. God notified a prophet named Samuel that the present king, Saul, failed to follow His commands, and that the next king would be one of Jesse's sons.

After Samuel interviewed seven of Jesse's sons, David was reluctantly called in from the field. Once David arrived, God told Samuel that the young shepherd boy, who spent most of his days alone taking care of sheep, was the anointed one.

God reminded Samuel that He does not look at outward appearances (the clothes we wear, the suits we have, or the cars we drive); He looks at the heart (1 Sam. 16:7). Immediately, Samuel anointed David king, not in the field or in a back room, but in front of his entire family.

As young as he was, one day David boldly took on the challenge to defeat an enemy of Israel named Goliath (1 Sam. 17:20–36). He rejected the sword, shield, and armor offered to him and used five stones and a sling as his weapon of choice. As David stood ready to battle one-on-one with Goliath, he reached into his bag and grabbed a stone. David then ran toward Goliath to muster momentum and slung the stone toward his forehead.

> God reminded Samuel that he does not look at outward appearances; He looks at the heart.

The precision and momentum must have been tremendous because that one stone sank into the forehead of its target, and Goliath fell like a rock (1 Sam. 17:48– 51). The young shepherd boy, who worked in the field, took Goliath's sword and killed him.

Unfortunately, David's victory over Goliath would be short-lived. As David's reputation grew, so did King Saul's jealousy. Saul did not appreciate the attention David was receiving and convinced himself that David was a serious threat to his throne. Saul's insecurities led him to one conclusion — David had to die.

David ran and hid from Saul for almost fifteen years after hearing that Saul wanted him dead. It was not until Saul died that David was finally free to take his place as king. It may take some time and patience, but if the promise can happen for David, it can happen for us.

> It may take some time and patience, but if the promise can happen for David, then it can happen for us.

Reflecting on my situation, it looked as though there was no way I would acquire the field technician job. I walked into the office believing the job was mine, but as the interview proceeded to the practical phase, things got complicated, and I began to doubt whether the job was really for me. I can imagine David's frustration as he tried to comprehend his suffering in the midst of his anointing.

Initially, it seemed as though David had gotten a raw deal on his anointed meal. Yet years later, with the promise fulfilled and his meal plan completed, David took his rightful place on the throne. Even when the unexpected occurs, the Head Chef's meal plans are coordinated with a purpose, timed to perfection, and served with love.

That is a spiritual meal all of us can look forward to consuming.

ENTRÉE #9

A Challenging Meal

The day was not supposed to end this way. I was looking forward to working out at the gym. As I made my way into the fitness center, I gave a shout-out to Ron, who was a regular at the gym. He worked out every day and was in great shape. I started to get into my routine, and sometime during my workout, Ron walked over to me and commented that I was not doing it correctly. I knew this brother for a long time, so I graciously told him thanks and kept going. Approximately fifteen minutes later, Ron walked over to me again and stated that I should change my routine. I was now asking myself, *What is wrong with this brother?*

We had different fitness goals. Ron focused on weight lifting, and my focus was on cardio. We never worked out with each other in all the years we had known each other, but we always respected each other's space. Therefore, I ignored him and stuck to my routine.

As he approached me one last time, I was not about to wait around for his next round of criticism. I left the fitness center and went to the locker room.

While I was preparing to go home, Ron entered the locker room and shouted, "If you were not so hard-headed, you would be much further along than you are." Then I turned my head and looked around to see who he was talking to. Unfortunately, when I looked back, there was nobody there but me!

So I asked him, "Are you talking to me?" He responded, "Yes, I am talking to you."

Now hold on. Let's back up a minute.

My wife sometimes tells me that I am too defensive, but in this case, I can justifiably state that I did nothing wrong. I knew this brother well. He was part of an assembly of men who were active in the community. We participated in local neighborhood events together and went to the same church. But none of that mattered. He was walking toward me, and he was upset.

For the next few minutes, he shouted and yelled about how I was not getting better results because I did not want to listen to him. His frustration started to boil over and we began to argue. Somewhere during the argument, I realized that the trash talking was escalating to the point of no return. What a picture: two Christian brothers on the brink of fighting in a locker room.

I wish I could tell you that there was some dramatic moment when I heard a "still small voice" tell me to cool out; however, that was not the case. At some point during all the chaos, I got control of my ego, shut my mouth, and walked away. Ron just stood there staring at me as I took my seat.

Without saying another word, I finished changing my clothes and left the gym. I spent the rest of the night reflecting on everything that had occurred. I wondered whether I could have responded to Ron's frustrations differently.

The following week, I saw Ron in the locker room. I did not say a word to him, nor did he say anything to me. After his workout, he approached me, held his hand out, and apologized. He explained that he was dealing with some personal issues, and I happened to be the unfortunate recipient of his frustration. In other words, I had been in the wrong place at the wrong time. I wanted to walk away and tell him it was too late, but I left it alone, shook his hand, and told him not to worry about it. "It's all good" (Rom. 8:28).

How should we respond to confrontation? Ron caught me off guard. Ultimately, this confrontation had nothing to do with me and everything to do with him. Despite who started it, I believe I could have responded to Ron in a better way. It is when we are tested that we can honestly access our spiritual maturity.

> It is when we are tested that we can honestly access our spiritual maturity.

There may be times when we will have to confront someone about an issue or circumstance. We can only hope that our response will coincide with our God given values when that situation occurs. I should have responded to Ron in a more humble manner. Our confrontation should have never reached the point where our actions failed to represent God's patience and understanding.

A prophet named Elijah had to prepare for a confrontation with a king who insisted on worshiping a false idol. According to Biblical records, no other king was as evil as Ahab (1 Kgs. 16:30). Elijah had to confront King Ahab for disobeying God's commands, but the confrontation had to be done according to God's timing. He warned King Ahab that judgment was coming because of his insistence on worshiping a false god (Baal).

> Just before Elijah would confront Ahab, God sent him into the wilderness.

Elijah was God's chosen prophet to bring redemption to a fallen nation. But right before Elijah could enact God's judgment on King Ahab, God sent Elijah alone into the wilderness (1 Kgs. 17:2–4). His time in the wilderness was no picnic. Elijah had to drink from a stream to get water and wait for birds to provide him with food. During his time in the wilderness, he had to wait on God and was totally dependent on God to survive. It was probably just the environment Elijah needed to refresh himself spiritually and prepare for the major confrontation headed his way.

Fresh out of the wilderness and empowered, Elijah was ready to battle. He told King Ahab to meet him on Mount Carmel and bring all 450 of the prophets of Baal with him. Ahab agreed, and the stage was set for an epic showdown.

The rules were as follows: Two bulls would be provided at Mount Carmel. Both Elijah and Ahab's prophets would cut the meat from their bulls and place it on their designated piece of wood. No fire would be placed under the wood. Ahab's prophets would be allowed to call on their god to burn their meat. Elijah would be allowed to call on the Lord to burn his meat. The first party to get their meat to burn wins.

> Everyone wants a powerful testimony, but not everyone want to go through the wilderness to get it.

The prophets of Baal went to work. They called on the name of Baal from morning to evening, and despite their efforts, Baal failed to respond. Elijah finally had enough. Now it was his turn. He called everyone over to his wood altar, saturated the wood with water, and then began to pray to the Lord.

As he finished praying, fire came down from the heavens, burned the meat and everything around it. The crowd was stunned. After witnessing the power of God, they fell to their knees, bowed down in fear, and shouted the Lord was the true God (1 Kgs. 18:38–39). It was a powerful biblical event in scripture and a definitive victory for the Lord.

This incredible show of spiritual authority may not have occurred if Elijah had not entered the wilderness. Waiting on God in the wilderness must have felt like an eternity for Elijah. However, in the end, Elijah proved that if we stay strong while we are in our wilderness, the Head Chef would show up, create a meal, and feed His people.

ENTRÉE #10

Delayed Service

I have been praying for a personal breakthrough for a while. Sometimes it appears that it is getting harder and harder to hear that "still small voice" that Elijah was talking about (1 Kgs. 19:12). I know that God is still here and that He still communicates with His people, but I often struggle to set aside the time required to tune in to His frequency. After all, my daily schedule tends to be scripted by a microwave society that refuses to slowdown.

Unfortunately, there are only twenty-four hours in a day, and five to six of those hours are designated for sleep (that is all I get most nights). Combine all this with email, web searches, text messages, and work-related tasks, and I have a recipe for a scheduling disaster.

Although I strive to provide some balance in my personal life, I am also aware that time management could be a critical element in enhancing my relationship with God. I was once challenged by someone who stated that we should not squeeze God into our busy schedules but should coordinate our daily schedule around His time. To be transparent, I have work to do in this area. However, do not judge me too harshly; we are all in the process of continual spiritual development.

The prophet Habakkuk was dedicated to worshiping the true and living God, but his heart was troubled. He had witnessed turmoil and chaos among his people. He questioned God's delay in restoring order and wanted answers. Habakkuk became fed up with waiting on God's timing.

> Habakkuk lost patience and became fed up with waiting on God's response.

Times were tough during Habakkuk's era. Judah, the southern division of Israel, was a nation spiraling down the path of disobedience and chaos. Habakkuk was distraught by the current state of events. What did he do when things were not going according to his expectations?

Habakkuk did not complain to his fellow prophets. He did not go on the internet to find out if other prophets felt the same way he did. He did not use social media to get feedback on his feelings. He went directly to God, frustrations and all, and asked Him why He was not doing anything to alleviate the rebellious atmosphere adversely affecting His people.

Habakkuk just put it out there and spoke from his heart. He asked God, "How long do I have to cry out to you and get no response? Why do you allow me to see evil, trouble, violence, strife and conflict and nothing is done to bring justice to our people?" (Hab. 1:1–4). It sounds like some of the same issues we face today.

In His time, God responded to Habakkuk. He assured Habakkuk that He was working things out for their good. He notified Habakkuk that judgment was on the way. God was going to send in a mighty army to punish the people of Judah for their disobedience. Habakkuk was praying for a breakthrough but not this type of breakthrough! What happens when God's response to our prayers does not meet our expectations?

> What happens when God's response to our prayers does not meet our expectations?

Stunned by God's response, Habakkuk asked God why He would use a mighty, ruthless army to correct His children. He challenged God on His plans and questioned His timing. God responded and promised Habakkuk that the wicked would not prosper for long (Hab. 2:3 NKJV). He promised Habakkuk that judgment would come to those who would harm His people. It may not have been what Habakkuk wanted to hear, but God answered his prayers.

So, what did Habakkuk do after hearing God's response? He decided to give God praise and summarized his encounter with God by stating, "Yet I will rejoice in the Lord, I will joy in the God of my salvation" (Hab.

3:18).

If there is one takeaway from Habakkuk's story, it is this: circumstances may not change overnight, but we can be assured that the Head Chef is working on our behalf and will respond to the concerns of His patrons at the appropriate time.

This is good news for those of us waiting and seeking answers to difficult circumstances.

ENTRÉE #11

Waiting for the Feast

After working out at the gym, my friend Shaw and I went to one of our favorite restaurants. We sat in the dining room and waited for our food to arrive. The dining room had a small yet lively crowd. There was a bar located on the other side of it. Things were going smoothly, and then suddenly, we heard someone shout from the bar, "Everyone go to the back and take everything out of your pockets!"

Without saying a word, Shaw looked at me, and I looked at him. There was a moment of silence as both of us paused to take in what we had just heard. Other customers in the dining room were concerned and began looking around for answers. I had no idea of what they were looking for, but I was not just going to sit there and analyze whether the threat was real or not.

Instinctively, Shaw and I jumped out of our seats, left the food on the table, and made our way toward the restaurant's exit. We were not wasting any time; we were out of there! As I passed the bar area, I heard it again, "Everyone go to the back and take everything out of your pockets!" I observed the staff looking mildly concerned.

I asked myself, *Didn't they hear what I just heard?* I thought, *something is not right.* I slowed down and cautiously walked toward the bar. At this point, I had no idea where Shaw had gone. As I entered the bar, everything seemed normal. Then I heard the disturbing voice that had disrupted my dinner.

A man was standing in a wobbly manner, talking loudly, and trying to hold steady the drink he had in his hand. Remarkably, I happened to know this guy, but I did not realize that drinking would cause him to completely lose it. I walked up to him and asked if he was out of his mind for yelling a statement like that in public. He smiled at me, glassy-eyed, as though nothing had happened, and stated, "Sorry, Ken, I was just joking."

I thought to myself, *really*? I just shook my head in amazement. I knew he would not be able to comprehend what was trying to say in his intoxicated state, so in frustration I shook my head and walked out of the bar. I found Shaw and told him that everything was cool. I told him that the threat was just someone at the bar who had too much to drink. We returned to our seats to wait for our meals. I did not know about Shaw, nor did I ask, but I had had enough for one evening. My tolerance for nonsense had been exhausted, and my patience was strained. Although my meal was on the way, I was ready to go home.

Like my experience in the restaurant, unexpected things can happen while we are waiting for our promised meals to arrive. Simeon may not have dealt with the type of drama that Shaw and I were confronted with, however, just like some of us, his patience may have been tested as he steadfastly trusted God to keep His word.

> Similar to my restaurant experience, unexpected things can happen while waiting on God's promises.

Simeon was a devout and righteous man waiting for the Messiah to come. His wait was justified because it was revealed to him that he would not see death until he had seen the Messiah (Lk. 2:26). Yet unbeknownst to Simeon, his life was about to change. His promised meal had arrived.

One day while Simeon was at the temple, Mary and Joseph arrived unexpectedly to present their child to the Lord (Lk. 2:22-35, Lv. 12). Incredibly, the Spirit led Simeon to the temple on the same day that Mary and Joseph were to dedicate Jesus to God. At that moment, Simeon took the child up in his arms, blessed God, and stated that he could now die in peace knowing that he had seen the Savior (Lk. 2:28–29).

Simeon finally received his opportunity to meet the Messiah, but I feel that he had even more to thank God for. God showed favor upon Simeon by sustaining him in his old age until God's promise was realized. We do not know how long Simeon had to wait, but scripture states that his character was undeterred despite the delay.

Unlike the frustration I exhibited in the restaurant as I dealt with that unexpected incident, Simeon gracefully waited on God's timing regardless of the unpredictable way that God served his meal. I was so aggravated with the circumstances at the restaurant that I missed out on my purpose for being there, to relax and enjoy a good meal after a hard workout.

> Simeon gracefully waited on God's timing regardless of the unpredictable way God fulfilled His promise.

Simeon's response reminds us that if we stay focused on God's promises, regardless of waiting and unforeseen circumstances, we will be able to experience the benefits of God's timing.

This is awesome news for those of us praying and waiting on God to serve the meals He created for us.

ENTRÉE #12

Feast for a King

The prophets predicted His existence. Many anticipated His coming. His suffering is documented in scripture. He was born under unreasonable circumstances and in substandard conditions. His life was at stake as soon as He entered the world. He relocated from town to town to ensure His existence.

At twelve years old, Jesus was sitting in the temple, talking with the teachers, listening, and asking questions. He grew in wisdom and stature. Although Jesus was knowledgeable, He did not start His ministry until He was thirty years old. He warned some individuals not to tell anyone about the help He gave them because of God's timing. After healing a man with leprosy, Jesus asked him not to speak to anyone because of God's timing (Mark 1:40–45). After turning water into wine, He told His mother that it was not time for Him to begin His work (Jn. 2:4). Jesus understood the importance of timing when it came to fulfilling God's will.

Timing was critical then and is still vital now. When my prayers are not answered in what I may perceive as a timely manner, I try to remind myself that God is still in control. "But when the fullness of the time was come, God sent forth His Son, made of a woman, made under the law" (Gal. 4:4).

To some, Jesus was the son of a carpenter, but history will record His arrival and mission as the ultimate example of God's perfect timing.

ENTRÉE #13

Get Up and Eat

It was a great time for family and friends to enjoy each other's company. The atmosphere was delightful, and the guests were in a festive mood. Then, the Guest of Honor arrived. When the word got out that Jesus was in town, everyone wanted to see Him. However, everyone's motives were not the same. Those who accepted Him came because they believed He was who He said He was. Some came just to see about His friend Lazarus. Others came to plot the death of both of them.

Whatever the reason, Jesus was the center of everyone's attention. While the crowd was growing outside, things were going well inside. As with life itself, this was the calm after the storm. Days prior to this celebratory dinner, the circumstances were gravely different.

Lazarus, who was a good friend to Jesus, was struck with a major illness. Therefore, it came as no surprise that Mary and Martha, Lazarus's sisters, would send an urgent message to Jesus to notify Him. When Jesus heard the news about Lazarus, one would assume that He would tell His apostles to prepare to take an urgent trip with Him to heal Lazarus. However, that was not the way it happened. Unexplainably at the time, not only did Jesus not rush to see His friend Lazarus, but He waited an additional two days before going to see him.

That inaction alone was enough for anyone to question Jesus' decision. Meanwhile, Lazarus probably did not anticipate that he would have to wait long for his healing. I can envision him looking out the window, waiting to see if Jesus was coming up the road. I can only imagine what his spiritual disposition might have been as each day went by.

> Lazarus probably did not anticipate that he would have to wait long for his healing.

While Lazarus's illness was likely worsening by the day, Jesus finally decided to make His way out to see him. Unfortunately, when Jesus arrived, He found out that Lazarus died and had been in the grave for four days.

While friends mourned with Mary and Martha over the death of their brother, Martha got the word that Jesus was in town. She ran to meet Him and stated, "Lord if You had been here, my brother would not have died. But even now I know that whatever You ask of God, God will give You" (Jn. 11:21–22 NKJV). I do not know if she was admonishing Jesus for His late arrival or making a declaration of faith. Maybe both.

Regardless, Jesus did not get defensive and did not explain why He was late. That is a lesson we can all apply to our lives when accusations come our way. Jesus responded to Martha, "Your brother will rise again" (Jn. 11:23 NKJV). As they approached the burial site, Jesus told the crowd to remove the stone from the grave.

It did not take much for Jesus to do what He came to do and defy human logic. Nor did it take many words for Jesus to prove that His timing was the best timing. He cried, "Lazarus, come forth!"

> It did not take much for Jesus to defy human logic and prove that His timing was the best timing.

The biblical book of John states what happened next, "And he who had died came out bound hand and foot with grave clothes, and his face was wrapped with a cloth. Jesus said to them, 'Loose him, and let him go'" (Jn. 11:44 NKJV). Jesus did the unexplainable and rose Lazarus from the dead!

Days later, there was a big celebration. Jesus was with His friend Lazarus and his sisters, Mary and Martha. One can only imagine the joyful atmosphere at Lazarus's home. After all, they'd experienced a miracle. It would have never happened if God's timing had not been in effect.

Even if we do not understand God's purpose, His timing will ultimately provide us with the perfect meals for our lives.

ENTRÉE #14

No Food in Sight

We had been dating exclusively for a year. We'd made it past the chicken Caesar salad incident (Entrée #6) and entered a new season. We felt comfortable with each other. We enjoyed each other's company. We went to church together. It was a time of promise, hope, and great expectations.

I was about to do my laundry and called her to see how she was doing. She was working on a project and could not talk on the phone for too long. Looking to impress her, I told her that I was in the process of doing my laundry and if she came over, I would take care of her laundry as well. She could finish her project at my house while her clothes were being washed. I told her it was a win-win proposal. She agreed.

She came over and gave me her laundry. My expectations were high as I knew she would give me major credit for correctly washing her clothes. It's one thing when associates and coworkers give us compliments for doing a good job, but it is another thing when your significant other or spouse gives you praise for doing something well; it takes the appreciation to another level.

She continued to work on her project as I went to the laundromat. I washed her clothes as though I were working on a technical project at my job. I silently guaranteed there would be no pink undershirts or underwear when I was done. I was determined for the outcome to meet her standards. I finished the job in less than two hours and was on my way back home.

My anticipation soared as I came up the driveway. I entered my house and announced with a big smile on my face that the laundry was done. She turned around from the computer monitor, smiled, and stated, "That's great."

Yes, I thought to myself; her reaction was what I hoped it would be. However, as she continued to look at me, her facial expression changed to a look of curiosity. Therefore, I knew something was on her mind.

I asked her, "What's wrong?" She hesitated to respond, so I asked her again, "What's wrong?"

She smiled at me and asked, "What did you do with the bag?"

I said, "Excuse me?"

She said, "What did you do with the laundry bag?" Now I was getting nervous. I was not ready for this.

I thought I had the laundry thing down to a science. In fact, I didn't even know why she was asking me this question. Who cares about what happens to the bag? So I carefully told her that the laundry bag with her clothes was in the living room.

She then asked, "Did you wash the bag?"

I nervously replied, "What?"

She inquired again, "Did you wash the laundry bag?"

I stated no.

Her next question is one I will remember for the rest of my life. She asked, "Why would you put clean clothes in a dirty bag?"

"What?" I was stunned. I just stared at her to buy some time to think of a response. Who would have thought about washing a laundry bag? After a minute or so, I came to terms with reality and reasoned that she was right.

She chuckled, gave me a hug, and graciously thanked me for washing her clothes. Then she turned around and continued to work on her project. I stood there for another minute as I tried to figure out what had just happened. We still had a great evening, but that laundry bag issue bothered me all week. So much for washing clothes and so much for my expectations.

What happens when our prayers are not answered in a way that we expect? The apostle Paul experienced this dilemma first handedly. He prayed and asked God for a response to a personal struggle he was dealing with. Yet God did not immediately respond to his prayers. Paul had to accept that there would not be a quick answer to his request. He had to come to terms with the fact that his meal would take some time to cook.

Whether it is a minor issue like my laundry or a significant problem, such as Paul's predicament, the struggle to accept responses that do not meet our expectations is a real challenge that many of us will have to contend with.

Paul was chosen by God, but this did not shield him from giving in to his ego. Paul knew he had to discipline himself so that the emphasis of his mission would always be God-centered. However, it appears God was not about to take any chances with Paul's ego. He allowed Paul to endure an affliction defined as "a thorn in the flesh" (2 Cor. 12:7). Even though the nature of Paul's hardship was not identified in scripture, it was so harsh that Paul could only go to God for relief.

> What happens when our prayers are not answered in the way we expect them to be?

Initially, it appears as if Paul did not accept his fate gracefully. In fact, he begged God to take the affliction away and patiently waited to hear from the Lord. It must have seemed like an eternity, but after his third plea for mercy, God replied and told Paul, "My grace is sufficient for you, for My strength is made perfect in weakness" (2 Cor. 12:9). That was it — short, direct, and to the point.

We should give Paul some credit. It was not the response he was hoping for, yet he accepted his fate and looked at his situation from a different perspective. Paul reasoned, "Therefore I take pleasure in infirmities, in reproaches, in needs, in persecutions, in distresses, for Christ's sake. For when I am weak, then I am strong" (2 Cor. 12:10).

Now that is spiritual maturity. Waiting was not easy for Paul and it is sure not easy for us. However, despite our fast-paced society and get-it-now mentality, good things do come to those who wait.

Are you full yet? You have ingested all fourteen entrées. Now it is time for dessert!

"If we patiently wait on God's timing, the Head Chef will always serve us a delightfully sweet treat that will satisfy our cravings and fulfill our desires."

CHAPTER 7
Dessert

Dining protocol indicates that our delightful dining experience is not complete without offering dessert. For some people, dessert significantly influences the rating of their dining experience. Knowing this, restaurants may highlight their dessert menu recognizing that these after-dinner treats can positively influence their customer's reviews.

It was late one night, and my friend Rochelle and I had been talking on the phone for a while. The conversation went from current events to social issues and from social issues to food. We talked about good meals and dining experiences. When we got to the topic of desserts, especially cheesecake, there was a heightened sense of enthusiasm in the air.

Have you ever thought about your favorite dessert so vividly that your mouth started to water? Well, that must have been the case with Rochelle because as we continued talking over the phone, I suddenly heard the roar of a car engine. She suddenly had the urge for dessert — not any dessert but red velvet cheesecake from a well-known establishment across town. The restaurant closed at midnight. I did not even get a chance to talk her out of it. She was determined to get that red velvet cheesecake.

Rochelle lived approximately twenty minutes away. She had ten minutes to find a parking space and enter the Promised Land flowing with milk and creamed cheese! Needless to say, she got her cheesecake seconds before the restaurant's doors closed. However, unlike Rochelle's experience, our spiritual desserts may require more time to receive.

David, the King of Israel, had just gotten out of bed. The cooler weather was probably just what he needed to gather his thoughts. David had a beautiful home that overlooked the landscape. As he surveyed the countryside, he was pleasantly distracted by a stunning sight.

From his roof, he saw a woman bathing. Her beauty far exceeded anything he expected to view from the rooftop of his home. He was a prominent man. His position allowed him to access the most beautiful women throughout the land. He had power and influence, and because of his authority, he demanded to find out her status.

He sent messengers to get some information on her status. The word came back that she was married, and her husband was a military commander who worked for him. However, none of that mattered now; he was obsessed with her beauty and, despite her marital status, made his move. She was notified of his interest and escorted to his home. She probably thought about her obligation to her husband. But it was too late. Bathsheba was now in the arms of David, and their worlds would never be the same.

He thought he had gotten away with his actions, but the evidence of his actions had become known as Bathsheba notified David that she was pregnant. David tried to figure out a way to cover up his actions. His ultimate plan was to have her husband placed on the front lines of the war, where there was heavy fighting. His death would be assured because of his close position in the battle. As planned, Bathsheba's husband died in combat, and she was free to become David's wife. Yet David's actions displeased God (2 Sam. 11:26).

> David was given everything he needed and maybe more, but he did evil in God's sight.

David was given everything he needed and maybe more, but he did evil in God's sight (2 Sam. 12:7). He killed an innocent man and took that man's wife. God's law stated the penalty for David's sins was death.

He knew he deserved his fate, and with a contrite heart, David repented (Ps. 51). In an amazing turn of events, God interrupted David's fate to fulfill His promise. God told David that He would forgive him for his sins and he would not die (2 Sam. 12:13).

David's future was destined when he was fifteen years old. His meal plan looked exceptional as he was prepared to eat at the Head Chef's table. However, David refused to follow his designated meal plan. He decided to engage in the dessert portion of his plan (Bathsheba) before receiving the entrée that the Head Chef had created.

> In an amazing turn of events, God interrupted David's fate to fulfill His promise.

The Head Chef was disappointed, but because David repented, God's ultimate plans were undeterred by David's sins. God kept His promise to create a meal that would last for generations to come. If we patiently wait on God's timing, the Head Chef will always serve us a delightfully sweet treat that will satisfy our cravings and fulfill our desires.

That, my friends, is a great reason to enjoy your dessert!

CHAPTER 8

Check and Gratuity

As for the dinner check and gratuity, Jesus paid the price for our meals a long time ago. The only thing we should do is accept His offer and go home knowing our meals were paid in full.

I will be forever grateful for a certain life-changing experience that highlights the perfection of God's timing. When I was sixteen, I joined a bowling league not far from my home. I was not a great bowler, but it was a way to get some exercise and meet some good people. While bowling, I met a charismatic brother named Junior. We bowled together for a couple of years, and then, for some reason, the league shut down. We lost contact with each other and moved on with our lives.

Eight years later, in an effort to keep my weight down, I joined a gym. I was working a full-time job during the day and going to school at night. My schedule was tight, and my frustrations started to get the best of me. Working out allowed me to release some unwanted energy.

As I became familiar with the regulars at the gym, one person, in particular, Mr. Brown, became a guiding force in my life. He educated me on the benefits of balancing my work and personal life. He also advised me on how to make sensible choices and told me to keep God first in my life. I soaked up every bit of knowledge he was willing to share.

A couple of years after I joined the gym, guess who showed up one day while I was working out — Junior. It was at that time, I learned that Mr. Brown was his father. What was the likelihood that after ten years of not talking to each other, the man mentoring me would be Junior's father? Junior and I kept in touch from that day on.

Years later, at a family event, Junior introduced me to his cousin. She was a God-fearing, attractive, educated woman who was down-to-earth, a total package that caught my interest. We spoke casually, but I had recently come out of a long-term relationship that did not end well, and I needed time to recover. I later found out that she also needed some time before getting into a relationship as well.

Fast forward 15 years; it was time to celebrate Mr. Brown's eightieth birthday. Everyone was at his party, including, guess who? — Junior's cousin! It had been years since we had seen each other. We were both single and my days of waiting for something to happen were over. I was not going to let another opportunity get away. I approached her, and we talked briefly. Not wasting any time, I smoothly slid her my business card and asked her to call me. She smoothly gave my card back to me and told me to call her. Now that's the kind of traditional move that I like! It did not take long for me to pick up the phone and pursue my destiny. Eighteen months after Mr. Brown's party, Dayema and I got married, and the rest is history.

Mr. Brown taught me how to manage my professional and personal life at a young age. Amazingly, at the time, he had no idea that he was grooming me to be a suitable husband for his niece. When I needed someone to speak on my behalf, he had no problem vouching for me because he knew what seeds he had planted in my life.

Yes, it took several years for his niece and I to come together, but that is all right; sometimes, the best meals take time!

"I have come to terms with the fact that waiting on God's timing may often be challenging."

CHAPTER 9

Food for Thought

I enjoyed our short journey together as we sought to understand God's timing. We explored some of the historical relationships that occurred between God and humankind. Since God is the same yesterday, today, and forever, we can surmise that God's patterns from the past are still in effect for this generation and the next. This should be of comfort to all of us seeking answers and patiently waiting for our meals to arrive.

The experiences of those mentioned in scripture illustrate how it can be a struggle to wait on God's timing. Yet, knowing that the Head Chef's menu is critical to our destiny is comforting. He will always have a seat for us at His table to enjoy the meals He promised us.

I appreciate you dining and engaging with me in a conversation about God's timing. A huge effort was made to ensure that the text was scripturally accurate, focused, and provided a read that all could enjoy. That said, I hope you read this book with an open heart, knowing that my goal was to be transparent in my pursuit to understand God's timing.

This kitchen is closing now, but the Head Chef restaurant is always open! He works twenty-four hours a day and seven days a week. He is always planning His next meal. His food can take some time to cook, but He promises to satisfy our appetites and fulfill our desires.

In the end, we can be comfortable knowing that God will never serve us food that is *cooked on the outside but raw on the inside.*

Blessings,
Ken

About the Author

Born in the projects of New York City, Ken Bosket, MSEM, Engr., uses life's challenges as a platform for success. Always thinking, Ken questioned the norms of society and wondered whether today's mindset could be effective in tomorrow's high-tech culture. His curiosity challenged him to evaluate the sometimes-conflicting relationship between spirituality and humanity. Ken decided to express his thoughts on paper and wrote his first book, *Cooked on the Outside, Raw on the Inside: The Struggle to Wait on God's Timing*, in 2018. Later, in an effort to understand his struggle to focus and retain information in today's high-tech society, Ken wrote his second book, In One Ear, Out the Other: Hearing the Word in a Microwave Society. Always reflecting, in a moment of uncertainty, Ken recently questioned whether his humanity and shortcomings could possibly become a roadblock to his purpose. After searching the Bible, he wrote his third book, *Flaw'ishing: You Don't Have to Be Perfect to Be Chosen"*. To keep his books reader-friendly, he displays a writing style that is a light-hearted mix of conversation, information, and thought-provoking dialog.

Is it possible to hear, absorb, and retain information in a digital age full of distractions? We live in a society that has embraced the use of smartphones, tablets, mobile apps, internet services, gaming consoles, social media, etc. Yet are these sources of convenience and entertainment a good thing? Even if the overall aspects of technology are beneficial, are we so far addicted to computers that its use has become an obstacle to God's purpose?

AVAILABLE ON AMAZON

www.cookedontheoutside.com
cookedontheoutside@gmail.com

www.ingramcontent.com/pod-product-compliance
Lightning Source LLC
Chambersburg PA
CBHW031454040426
42444CB00007B/1097